Date Due

AP 11 '00			
			·
	·		

BRODARi   Cat. No. 23 233   Printed in U S A

POPULAR CULTURE IN AMERICA

1800-1925

POPULAR CULTURE IN AMERICA

1800-1925

Advisory Editor
DAVID MANNING WHITE

Train Robberies
Train Robbers
.........AND.........
The "Holdup" Men

William A[llan] Pinkerton, *1846 - 1923,*
"

ARNO PRESS
A New York Times Company
New York • 1974

Reprint Edition 1974 by Arno Press Inc.

Reprinted from a copy in the State Historical
Society of Wisconsin Library

POPULAR CULTURE IN AMERICA: 1800-1925
ISBN for complete set: 0-405-06360-1
See last pages of this volume for titles.

Manufactured in the United States of America

———◆———

Library of Congress Cataloging in Publication Data

Pinkerton, William Allan, 1846-1923.
    Train robberies, train robbers, and the "hold-up" men.

    (Popular culture in America)
    Reprint of the 1907 ed.
    1. Train robberies. 2. Brigands and robbers.
I. Title. II. Series.
HV6652.P55 1974   364.1'55   74-15748
ISBN 0-405-06383-0

Train Robberies
Train Robbers
.........AND.........
The "Holdup" Men

ADDRESS BY

WILLIAM A. PINKERTON

ANNUAL CONVENTION

International Association Chiefs of Police

JAMESTOWN, VA.

1907

COMPLIMENTS OF
WILLIAM A. PINKERTON, Chicago,
ROBERT A. PINKERTON, New York.

NOVEMBER, 1907

WILLIAM A. PINKERTON.

The late ROBERT A PINKERTON.

"HANDS UP."

ERETOFORE my addresses have been upon sub-
jects with which most of us are familiar and, while
I know there are among those present, members
of this Association who have had more or less to
do with the apprehension of the train robber or "hold-up"
criminal, a product we have that no other country has except as our fugitives; I believe some reminiscences of
these outlaws will be of interest.

As the detective agents throughout the United States of
many railroad, express and stage companies and of the
American Bankers' Association, and co-operating with police officials, United States marshals, sheriffs, railroads detectives and various other law enforcement authorities, for
over fifty years our agency has been engaged investigating
many of the robberies of railroad trains, banks and stages
by this desperate robber; my father, the late Allan Pinkerton, my brother Robert and I, often in these years person-
ally taking part in running down this now almost extinct
outlaw. It is somewhat remarkable as will be noted
throughout my talk, that in many instances brothers were
members of individual bands, notably the Reno brothers,
John, Frank, Sim and Bill; the Reitenhouse brothers; the
Miles brothers, James K. and Joe, all of Indiana; the
Farrington brothers, Levy and Hillary, of West Tennessee; the James brothers, Frank and Jesse; the Younger
brothers, Cole, Jim, John and Bob; the Logan brothers,
Harvey and Lonny; the Collins brothers, part of the Sam
Bass gang, Joel, William and Albert; Bud and William

Mc Daniels, part of the Jesse James gang; the Dalton brothers, Bill, Bob, Emmett and Gratton of Kansas; the Burrows brothers, Rube and Jim of Alabama; the Sontag brothers, John and George of Minnesota; the Gates brothers of California; the Jones brothers; the McCarthy brothers, Tom and Bill of Colorado; the Cook brothers, Bill and Jim of Arkansas, who were part of the Dalton gang and the Carver and Kilpatrick brothers of Texas.

The "hold-up" robber originated among bad men of the gold mining camps. Unsuccessful as a prospector, too lazy to work, and with enough bravado and criminal instinct to commit desperate crimes, he first robbed prospectors and miners en route on foot to stage stations, of their gold dust and nuggets, becoming bolder, looting stages and eventually after the railroads were built, he "held-up" railway trains and robbed express cars.

We also find them from the "dare-devils" of the Civil War, those from the Southwest who engaged in guerrilla warfare, where, as the pride of the States which sent them to the front and, because of their ambuscades, raids and lawless acts during the war, they were received as heroes when they returned to their homes. The James boys, the Youngers, the Renos, the Farringtons, the war giving them the reckless life they longed for and experience fitting them for the life of crime they inaugurated immediately after.

In the early days of the plains, the cowboy, with criminal inclination, noted for deeds of daring, began his career by cattle "rustling" and horse stealing, and then became a "hold-up" of stages and trains, committing the most of these robberies since 1875.

Also certain sensational newspapers and publishers of "yellow" covered literature, by exploiting and extoling the cowardly crimes of these outlaws and filling the youthful mind with a desire for the same sort of notoriety and adventure are responsible for many imitators of the "hold-up" robber.

The "hold-up" man operated as the footpad does to-day, concealed in ambush awaiting his victim, suddenly pouncing upon and commanding him to throw up his hands, "covering" him by thrusting a revolver in his face, then relieving him of his money and valuables. Usually the "hold-up" man to avoid identification and arrest, covers his face below the eyes with a triangular cloth or pocket handkerchief, tied back of the head, wore a soft hat well down over his eyes, although in many of the great train and bank robberies shortly after the war, no masks of any kind were worn.

The average train robbery band formerly consisted of from five to eight men, but in recent years successful robberies have been committed by from three to five men and in a few instances by a lone individual.

Usually in these train robberies, one member of the band, with red lantern or flag, at a lonely spot would signal the train to a standstill, or one or two would board the "blind end" of a baggage or express car and nearing the point selected for the robbery, would climb over the tender into the locomotive, "cover" the engineer and fireman.

while others of the bandits uncoupled the express or money car and forced the engineer to carry them a mile or two distant, where the cars and safes would be forced open with dynamite. Resistance usually resulted in the death of those who interfered. Our study of the murders committed by these desperadoes shows fully 90 per cent to be assassinations, those killed generally being defenseless, or the outnumbering desperadoes by pouncing on their victims when least expected, giving them no chance for their lives.

Escapes were usually made with horses in waiting, in charge of a confederate at the place of the robbery, and often with relays of horses previously arranged, for covering five or six hundred miles, until they arrived at their homes or hiding places.

There is no crime in America so hazardous as "hold-up" robbery. Over two-thirds of those who have been engaged in these crimes, were killed while operating, or in resisting arrest, or from their wounds, lynched by posses, or as is known "died with their boots on," while nearly all others were either captured or sentenced to long terms of imprisonment or driven from the United States, becoming exiles in distant foreign climes. Those at large are constantly in fear of arrest, living secluded lives, and risking no chances of discovery by communicating with friends.

Shortly after the close of the Civil War there was an epidemic of train robberies in Indiana, especially between Indianapolis and New Albany on the Jeffersonville and Indianapolis R. R., now part of the Pennsylvania Railway System. My father, representing the Adams Express Company, who were the principal losers in these raids, and who had determined to disband this "hold-up" band, undertook this difficult task. It was early determined that the robberies were perpetrated by a desperate gang who made Seymour and the adjacent town of Rockford their headquarters, practically under the leadership of the Reno brothers, whose parents, hard working and respectable had settled on an Indiana farm years before and raised a family of five boys, John, Clinton, Sim, Bill and Frank, and a girl, Laura. During the later part of the Civil War all of the brothers, except Clinton, known as "Honest Reno," began criminal careers with the Reitenhouse brothers, James K. and Joe and Miles and John Ogle, counterfeiters, and Peter McCartney, an expert safe burglar, all of whom, as bounty jumpers, had swindled the Government out of large sums of money. At the close of the War, the Renos and their associates had returned to their homes at Seymour, Indiana, with plenty of money, dissipating, gambling and indulging in other vicious dissoluteness. Other younger men in their neighborhood, observing these reckless expenditures, naturally desired to likewise acquire money quickly and soon with the Renos and their confederates, including Albert Sparks, Henry Moore, John Gerrold and Thomas Henry, formed "hold-up" bands for robbing express messengers on railroads near Seymour. Robbery after robbery followed, arrests were numerous, but powerful influences and desperate intimidations by the criminals and their friends made their conviction practically impossible. Farmers supposed to be inimical to the band were terrorized, by their cattle being poisoned or maimed and their homes and barns burned until a reign of terror actually existed all over Southern Indiana.

The Renos met their first Waterloo during the Winter of 1867 and 1868. John Reno had robbed the county treasurer's office at Gallatin, Mo., of $20,000 and returned to Seymour, Ind., the stronghold of his criminal brothers, and where he considered he was safe. But on plans arranged by my father for a certain day, John Reno was decoyed by one of our secret operatives to the Seymour depot for the arrival of a through train, on which a Missouri Sheriff with six deputies arrived and pounced upon Reno and pulled him aboard. There was no time for Reno's usual savior, the writ of habeas corpus, or any other legal technicality to prevent his removal; a good friend had looked after the telegraph wires so that no detaining despatches could head off the train and John Reno was landed over the Indiana line into Jail at Gallatin, Mo., where he was soon convicted and sentenced to 20 years in the Missouri Penitentiary, serving every day of his sentence.

During the Winter of 1868, there were heavy robberies of safes of county treasurers' offices in Western Iowa, the last occurring at Glenwood, Mills Co., Iowa, when $20,000 was stolen. Our investigations had determined the criminals to be Frank Reno, Al Sparks, Miles Ogle and Mike Rogers, the last named a wealthy land owner of Council Bluffs, a pillar of the Methodist Church and highly respected in his community. Following a robbery at Magnolia, Har risonville, we had traced the robbers to Council Bluffs, where a watch on Rogers' house resulted in the capture, the day after the Glenwood robbery of the criminals named, the proceeds of the raid still in their possession, they quickly shoved it into a kitchen stove, from which we recovered it partially burned. They were all taken to Glenwood, Iowa, but on April 1, 1868, broke jail and fled, Frank Reno going to Windsor, Canada, where he became associated with Charles Anderson, a clever burglar and general criminal and with him eventually returned to Seymour.

Shortly after the Glenwod robbery, Walker Hammond, afterwards noted as a counterfeiter, and Mike Colleran, of Seymour, "held-up" an express messenger on a Jeffersonville railroad train, robbing him of $15,000 only to be "held-up" by the Reno brothers and relieved of their plunder. Hammond and Colleran were convicted and sentenced to long terms of imprisonment in the Indiana State Penitentiary.

Subsequently Frank, Sim and Billy Reno, with Miles Ogle and Charles Anderson, heavily armed, "held-up" a train near Seymour, threw the messenger into a ditch from the moving train and robbed the Adams Express Company's safe of $90,000. For this crime, Anderson and Frank Reno were arrested at Windsor, Canada, and after a contest lasting all Summer, were remanded for extradition and later in charge of Pinkerton detectives were lodged in the New Albany, Ind., jail. Meanwhile, Sim and Billy Reno were arrested in Indianapolis, Ind., and also lodged in the same jail. Henry Moore, Gerrold and Sparks and an unknown

MILES OGLE.
One of the first train robbers.   Member Reno Band "Hold ups."

man who "held-up" and robbed the J. M. & I. R. R. had been arrested at Seymour, and while enroute to the Brownstone jail were forcibly taken from their escorts and lynched by excited citizens who had become incensed at the outrages the Renos and their associates were committing.

This was followed by a Vigilance Committee, supposed to have come from the neighborhood of Seymour, visiting the New Albany jail, battering in the doors, over-powering the guards and hanging Frank, Sim and Billy Reno and Charles Anderson in the jail corridor. Notices were also posted in public places about Seymour, naming 25 people supposed to be affiliated with the Renos and warning them that if any house, cattle or other property was destroyed, the Committee would "meet" but once more to clean out the friends of the Renos remaining in the community. These drastic, though apparently necessary measures stopped train robbery in Southern Indiana; there has not been a train robbery there since and the identity of the Vigilantes is still a secret.

———

The State of Missouri has probably produced more train robbers than any other state in the Union and of whom the James brothers were the most desperate and vicious.

Among the Kentuckians who settled in Clay County, Mo., before the War were Doctor and Mrs. Samuels and their sons, Frank and Jesse James, sons of Mrs. Samuels' previous marriage. When the War broke out, the brothers joined the Quantrell band in their guerrilla warfare. After

JESSE JAMES.

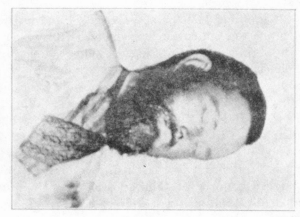

JESSE JAMES.
[after death.]

17

the War the James boys, under the leadership of Bill Anderson and operating with Cole, Jim, John and Bob Younger, Clell and John Miller, Charles Pitts, the Tompkins brothers, Jim Cummings, Dick Liddell, and other members of Quantrell's band, began prowling through West and Southwest Missouri and Eastern Kansas, looking for what spoils they could get and for years committed a series of the most despicable crimes of that period in Missouri, Kentucky and Minnesota, "holding-up" banks in the day time, robbing trains at night, murdering respectable citizens who resisted them and killing officers who attempted their arrest.

The published reports of the exploits of this band had more to do with the making of bad men in the West than anything which occurred before they began operating or since.

At the time Jesse James was killed and his brother surrendered the statement was made that neither was ever arrested or captured by officers, State or Federal, but Judge Philander Lucas of Liberty, Mo., states that during 1865-1866, about eleven o'clock one morning, the James boys, with Clell Miller, Jim Poole and George White, rode into Liberty, firing off their revolvers and acting like a lot of Indians; that they entered Meffert's saloon, had drinks, and as they left the saloon Sheriff Rickards arrested and disarmed the James boys, marched them into the Court House, arraigned them before him and that he committed them to the County jail. As a matter of fact, there were then no charges against them.

COLE YOUNGER.
[James Band.]

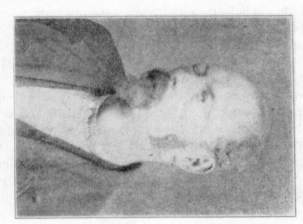

COLE YOUNGER.
After Northfield, Minn., bank raid.

As a rule the James and Younger brothers and their associates, after each crime, would return to their home, Clay County, Mo., where they were virtually immune from arrest, either through fear of them by the respectable element or through the friendly aid they received from their admirers.

The first of their robberies we were retained to investigate was that of June 3, 1871, when the James and Younger brothers visited Corydon, Wayne County, Iowa, intending to rob the county treasurer of recently collected taxes. Jesse James entered the treasurer's office offering a one hundred dollar bill for change, but the clerk informed him of the absence of the county treasurer, who held the combination of the locked safe, but suggested that a new bank across the square, opened that day and which had one-half of its capital on deposit, might accommodate him, where upon Jesse consulted with his associates and the robbery of the new bank was agreed upon. On Jesse offering the one hundred dollar bill, the cashier opened the safe for the change, only on turning around to look into the muzzle of two revolvers. Jesse's associates who had meanwhile entered the bank, then forced the president and cashier into a back room, emptied the contents of the safe, about fifteen thousand dollars into saddle bags, relieved a new depositor, a negro preacher, who had entered, of his handful of money, then mounting their horses fled from the town, passing on their way a public meeting, in the outskirts, where a site for a new school house was being discussed, and which

CHARLIE PITTS.
[James band.]

CHARLIE FORD.
[brother of "Bob" who killed Jesse James.]

accounted for the county treasurer's absence from his office, and saved his safe from being plundered.

As the bandits rode by the meeting they fired, in the air, a fusillade from their revolvers and rifles, at the same time informing the gathering of the robbery of the bank and advising that they return to town and start a new bank.

Robert Pinkerton, then a young man, with a posse traced the outlaws through the lower counties of Iowa. Then with an Iowa Sheriff, the balance of the posse having withdrawn, continued into Missouri as far as Cameron Junction, a cross road station, where the Sheriff left for additional help; but Robert Pinkerton continued following the trail to the Missouri River where the band separated, some crossing at Sibley Ferry, others at Blue Mill Ferry, all meeting afterwards at the Old Blue Mill, from which point they continued South, evidently making towards the James home in Clay County. Here, Robert Pinkerton, recognizing the folly of continuing alone withdrew.

On July 20, 1873, the James brothers committed their first train "hold-up" robbery on the Chicago, Rock Island & Pacific R. R., wrecking the train fifteen miles east of Council Bluffs, Iowa, murdered the unarmed engineer, wounded the fireman, injured passengers and robbed the express car of a large amount of money.

January 31, 1874, the James brothers aided by the Younger brothers, Clell Miller and Jim Cummings, committed their second train "hold-up" robbery, this, on the Iron Mountain Road at Gadshill, Mo., flagging the train to a standstill and "hold-up" and robbing it of $10,000. In

22

CLELL MILLER and BILL CHADWELL.
[James band.]
Killed by posse after Northfield, Minn. bank raid.

the investigation of this robbery Joseph W. Witcher, one of our detectives from Chicago, on March 10, 1874, was overpowered, bound with ropes and put on a horse, Clell Miller and Jesse James taking him from their home in Clay County, Mo., to near Independence, Jackson County, Mo., where they assassinated him, leaving his body at the crossing of the Deerington and Independence road where the Iowa Sheriff left Robert Pinkerton three years before.

A few days later Louis Lull, a former captain of police in Chicago, but then in our employ, in company with an ex-Deputy Sheriff and a man named Daniels, met John and Jim Younger on a road near Montegaw Springs, St. Clair County, Mo., and in the effort to arrest them, Lull killed John Younger, but was himself mortally wounded, dying six weeks later. Daniels was killed and Jim Younger was seriously wounded.

The James brothers band also committed robberies on the Union Pacific R. R., at Munsey, Kas., in December, 1875, securing $55,000, also on the Missouri Pacific R. R. at Otterville, Mo., July 8, 1876, securing $17,000, and when McDaniels, one of the band being arrested with part of the booty, was killed in an attempt to escape.

———

Their next serious crime was in September, 1876, when they attempted to rob a bank at Northfield, Minn., and killed the cashier, J. L. Haywood. Citizens of the town opened fight and killed Bill Chadwell, Clell Miller and Charley Pitts. Bob and Jim Younger and Jesse James

24

BOB YOUNGER.
[James band.]

JIM YOUNGER.
[James band.]

25

were wounded. Cole Younger picked up Bob and carried him away on his horse. A few days later, Cole, Jim and Bob Younger, surrounded in a swamp, were captured.

Frank James managed to get Jesse into Dakota and thence to the Missouri River, where they stole a skiff and made their escape.

Cole, Jim and Bob Younger were sentenced to long terms of imprisonment in the Shelwater, Minn., State Prison.

September 16, 1899, Bob Younger died in prison.

July 10, 1901, Cole and Jim Younger were pardoned by the Minnesota State Board of Pardons. October 18, 1902, Jim Younger committed suicide at St. Paul, Minn.

April 3, 1882, Bob Ford, a former associate of the James boys, for a reward of $10,000 offered by Gov. Crittendon for Jesse's body dead or alive, killed him while he was hanging a picture in his home at St. Joseph, Mo. Bob and Charles Ford surrendered themselves for this crime and were convicted and sentenced to death, but pardoned by Governor Crittendon and paid the $10,000; thus to Governor Crittendon is due the final disbanding of the James brothers band of outlaws and in this he was aided by Sheriff Timberlake of Clay County and Commissioner of Police Craig of Kansas City.

Frank James afterwards surrendered to the Missouri authorities, stood trial, and was acquitted of the Gallatin, Mo., bank robbery. Governor Crittendon refused to surrender him to the Minnesota authorities, and he subsequently settled in Western Missouri, and so far as I know, is now living a straightforward life.

Jesse James and the Youngers are all buried at the scenes of their boyhood days in Western Missouri.

Charley Bullard, alias "Piano Charley" and "Ike" Marsh, alias "Big Ike", who first came into prominence as "hold-up" robbers, have had rather an interesting career.

In 1869, Bullard and Marsh concealed themselves in a Hudson River R. R. train between New York City and Buffalo, "held-up", bound and gagged the messenger of the Merchants Union Express Co., and stole one hundred thousand dollars.

Bullard and Marsh were arrested in Canada, extradited and lodged in the White Plains, N. Y., jail for trial, from which, aided by "Billy" Forrester, an old-time associate, they escaped.

November 20, 1869, Bullard and Marsh with Adam Worth and "Bob" Cochran, stole from the Boylston Bank, Boston, Mass., cash and securities, valued at four hundred and fifty thousand dollars and fled to Europe with their plunder.

At the Washington Hotel, Liverpool, Bullard met and married a beautiful bar maid named Kittie Flynn, went to Paris, opened the famous American bar at Rue Scribe, where his wife's beauty and engaging manners attracted many American visitors as well as making it the headquarters of American gamblers and criminals who here planned many of their European crimes.

Bullard was, however, eventually, arrested and after a sentence of one year in Paris for keeping a gambling house, returned to the United States, was arrested in New York City for the Boylston Bank robbery and sentenced to twenty years in the State's prison at Concord, Mass., from which he escaped September 13, 1878, and fled to Canada, where he was arrested for a safe burglary and sentenced to five years imprisonment at Kingston. After serving this, he went abroad and with Max Shinburn, the notorious bank burglar, was arrested in the act of robbing a Bank at Viveres, Belgium. Bullard was sentenced to seventeen years imprisonment, in the Belgium penitentiary, where he died in the early part of 1890. Bullard was well educated, spoke English, French and German, fluently; was a skillful pianist, from which he gained the sobriquet of "Piano Charley."

After the Boylston Bank robbery, "Ike" Marsh separated from Bullard and with George Mason burglarized the First National Bank of Wellsboro, Pa., for which he was arrested, convicted and sentenced to seventeen years imprisonment in the Eastern Penitentiary, Philadelphia. While there he became a stationary engineer, and after his release, having reformed, followed his vocation as an engineer in Philadelphia, and is still so employed there.

In the early seventies, Levy and Hillary Farrington, from near Gilliam Station, West Tennessee, William Taylor,

William Barton, formerly a railroad brakeman and George Bertine, all from Western Tennessee, commenced train "hold-up" robberies on the Nashville and Northwestern and Mobile and Ohio Railroads, and after each "hold-up" the only trace of the robbers would be a skiff, left by the bandits floating bottom up on the Mississippi.

On the 6th of October, 1871, a train on the Mobile and Ohio R. R. at Union City, Tenn., was attacked, the guard and messenger overpowered and the safe of the Southern Express Company robbed of $20,000. I was then supervising for our Agency, all train robbery cases, and with Patrick Connell, Special Agent of the Southern Express Co., and an assistant named Bedlow, traced the men, as usual, to the Mississippi River, where an over-turned skiff was found and trace lost. After a most thorough scouring of the country and up and down the Mississippi River, we learned of a party of strange men in a swamp near Lester's Landing, Tenn., where we subsequently determined, they, to cover their real business of train robbery, had opened a small store. This we surrounded and attacked; the train robbers, who were heavily armed resisting and in the resulting fight, Henry Bertine was killed and Hillary Farrington and William Barton escaped. Hillary Farrington, we traced to Western Missouri, near Vinita, on the edge of Indian Territory, where with the aid of a deputy sheriff and some residents of the neighborhood, we surrounded the house in which he was secreted, but finally had to set fire to it in order to dislodge and arrest him.

A few days later Levy Farrington was arrested near Farmington, Ills., by the City Marshal and Robert A. Pinkerton, while William Taylor, the last of the band, was arrested by Patrick Connell and myself at Real Foot Lake, Tenn., and all taken to Union City, Tenn., for examination. When Levy Farrington arrived here in the custody of Robert A. Pinkerton, a friend named Toler, in attempting his rescue, shot and killed the Assistant City Marshal and seriously wounded a railroad watchman at Union City. Toler was pursued and captured and a Vigilance Committee was formed. Recognizing what might take place, we succeeded in getting Barton and Taylor out of the hotel where they were confined and heavily guarded, to the Memphis, Tenn., jail, but being unable to get the other prisoners away, the Vigilance Committee overpowered the local officers who were guarding them and that night shot and killed Levy Farrington and lynched Toler.

Taylor and Barton afterwards pleaded guilty to train robbery and were sentenced to long terms in the State Prison at Nashville, Tenn.

For very many years after train robbery in West Tennessee was an unknown crime.

In 1877, Sam Bass, Frank Hulfish, William Nixon, Henry Underwood and James Berry, a gang of cowboys, under the leadership of Joel Collins, near Big Springs, Neb., "held-up" a Union Pacific R. R. train, stealing $60,000 in gold, with which they started on horseback for Texas. Joel Collins, son of a preacher, came from near Dallas, Texas, and was one of four brothers, all of whom went wrong except Joe, who was a prominent respectable cattleman. Collins and Hulfish, ten days after the robbery near Ellsworth, Kas., and resisting arrest by United States troops were shot and killed; the money they carried with them was recovered. About two weeks later Jim Berry, who was traced to a farm near Mexico, Mo., was also shot and killed resisting arrest. Bass, Nixon and Underwood escaped, Nixon sailing from New Orleans, La., to Spanish Honduras, where he is still a fugitive and where he invested his share of the robbery, $10,000 gold, in business.

We located and caused the arrest of Henry Underwood and returned him to Kearney, Neb., where he escaped from jail and was last heard from as in the Indiana State Prison.

Sam Bass returned to Denton Co., Tex., where he has been a deputy Sheriff, and had many friends. He soon organized another band of train robbers, consisting of William and Albert Collins, brothers of Joel, James Pikes, Joe Herndon, of the Collins homestead, Henry Jackson and "Arkansas Johnson." They attacked the Southern Express Co., on the Texas and Pacific R. R. and the Houston and Texas Central R. R. and in the fall of 1877 committed a robbery at Mesquit, near Dallas, Texas. We co-operated with the local authorities and Texas rangers, resulting in the arrest of William Collins, Pikes and Herndon, the latter two were convicted at Tyler, Texas, and sentenced to life imprisonment in the United States Penitentiary at Detroit, Mich.

JAMES BURROWS.   RUBE BURROWS.

Alabama countrymen who became sensational Southern Express robbers.

32

Bill Collins forfeited his bond, but was located at Pembina, Minn., working as a cowboy. When Joseph Anderson, Deputy U. S. Marshal from Dallas, Texas, attempted to arrest him, both fired simultaneously, killing each other.

Albert Collins and "Arkansas Johnson" were killed resisting arrest. Sam Bass, with a confederate, was decoyed to Round Rock, Tex., by a friend, Jim Murphy, to rob a bank and was surrounded by Texas rangers and detectives, the Sheriff and his deputies; the effort to arrest them resulting in the killing of Bass and his companion. Jim Murphy, the "stool-pigeon," escaped unhurt, only to die shortly after collecting his reward, and is said to have been poisoned by friends of the Collins. Frank Johnson became a fugitive from justice and is supposed to have settled in Montana under an assumed name.

———

In 1888, Rube and Jim Burrows, originally from Vernon, Lamar County, Alabama, with W. L. Brock, all of whom had been railroad employees, farm-hands and cowboys, robbed the St. Louis, Arkansas and Texas Pacific Ry. in Texas, for which Brock was arrested and confessed, implicating the Burrows brothers. The Burrows boys returned to Montgomery, Ala., where they were arrested. While en route to the police station, Rube began firing and escaped. Jim, however, was overpowered and taken to Arkansas for trial for train robbery at Genowa, that state, and died in jail.

Rube Burrows kept in hiding until 1893, when he "held-

W. L. BROCK.
Associate of Rube and Jim Burrows.

up" a train on the Illinois Central Ry., near Sardis, Miss. He was subsequently killed by a posse, searching for him, in Middle Florida. Brock served a short term in the penitentiary.

In 1891, after the train left Tower Grove, a suburb of St. Louis, two masked men boarded the "blind" end of the express car, crawled over the tender and forced the engineer and firemen to stop the train at a cut near Old Orchard, where two additional men, also masked, boarded the rear end of the car. The messenger refused their demand to open the side door of the car, turned down the light, secured his revolver and began defending his trust. Immediately a heavy explosion occurred, tearing the car to pieces and filling the air with flying debris, a piece of which struck the messenger in the hip, knocking the revolver from his hand. Then the robbers, entered, opened the safe with nitro-glycerine, taking the contents, $10,000, and escaped. Co-operating with Lawrence Harrigan, then Chief of Police, and William Desmond of the detective department of St. Louis, Mo., we determined the "hold-ups" to be Marion C. Hedgepeth, a notorius Western outlaw, James Francis, a St. Louis burglar, Dink Wilson, an Omaha burglar, and Adelbert Sly of St. Joe, Mo., at one time a driver for the American Express Co., and who had stolen $20,000 from them. We learned Sly had gone to Los Angeles, and there Robert A. Pinkerton, aided by Detective Whittaker of San Francisco and Detective Hawley of Los Angeles arrested

MARION HEDGSPETH.
Stole $10,000 from St. Louis & San Francisco express.

him and later the San Francisco police, after a desperate struggle arrested Hedgepeth in that city. Hedgepeth and Sly were returned to St. Louis, convicted and sentenced to 20 years imprisonment. Sly is now at Liberty, but Hedgepeth, after his release continued his life of crime. [Is now, October, 1907, awaiting trial at Council Bluffs, Iowa, for a safe burglary there on September 1, 1907.] Francis was killed near Pleasandon, Kas., resisting arrest. Wilson shot and killed Detective Harvey of Syracuse, N. Y., for which he was electrocuted at Sing Sing Prison, N. Y., and his brother Charley, who was with Dink when Detective Harvey was killed, who we located in Buffalo, N. Y., and caused his arrest, was sentenced to prison for life.

In 1891, at Western Union Junction on the Chicago, Milwaukee & St. Paul R. R. not far from Racine, Wis., a train was "held-up" and on the express messenger refusing to surrender the express car was attacked with dynamite, literally blowing the safe to pieces and the messenger barely escaped with his life.

Later at Mankato, Minn., on the Northern Pacific R. R. a similar robbery was attempted. The identity of the "hold-ups" in these two robberies was unknown, but in the latter case, two suspects having purchased tickets for California via Portland, Ore., we, by telegraphing the numbers of these tickets and descriptions of the suspects to our Portland, Ore., office the suspects were put under surveillance, located at Visalia, Cal., and identified as John and George Sontag, brothers, originally from Mankato, Minn., who

37

GEORGE SONTAG.   Stage Train and Express robbers.   JOHN SONTAG.

38

had joined Chris Evans, an associate. Our watching of them developed the fact of their purchasing dynamite, and other circumstances towards verifying the suspicion against them, but not establishing evidence to act upon, our surveillance was stopped for the time being.

At Collins Station, Fresno Co., Cal., August 3, 1892, a Southern Pacific R. R. train was "held-up", the express car dynamited and $2,300 stolen. With the information of our previous investigation the railroad detectives and express special agents established the fact that the robbers were the men we had followed to Visalia, Cal., and an attempt to arrest them resulted in one of the officers being killed, another dangerously wounded, and the bandits escaping. A regular man-hunt, one of the most exciting that ever occurred on the Pacific Coast followed for months through the mountains of California, resulting finally in the arrest of George Sontag, who, forty hours after was sentenced to life imprisonment in the Folsom, Cal., Penitentiary. Several months afterwards John Sontag and Chris Evans were captured, after a long and desperate fight with a posse, both were badly wounded, Evans losing his right eye and one arm.

John Sontag died in jail, soon after his arrest. Evans was sentenced to life imprisonment, but escaped from jail at Fresno, December 28, 1893; was recaptured, February 18, 1894, and is now serving a life sentence in the Folsom, Cal., prison.

CHRIS EVANS.
Associate of Sontag Bros.

The Dalton brothers, Bill, Bob, Emmett and Grattan, committed a series of robberies in Missouri, Arkansas, Indian Territory, Oklahoma and California, from February, 1891, to May, 1894, operating with Joe Evans, "Texas Jack," Tom Littleton, Jim Wallace, Charles White and Jim Jones. They "held-up" a train on the Southern Pacific R. R. at Alila, Tulare County, California, killed the express messenger and fireman; "held-up" the Wells Fargo Express at Red Rock, Indian Territory, "held-up" a Missouri, Kansas and Texas passenger train at Adair, Indian Territory, securing the contents of the Pacific Express Co.'s safe.

At Coffeyville, Kansas, on October 5, 1892, one band attempted to rob a private bank, while the other made a similar attack on the First National Bank. The cashier of the former temporized with the bandits by telling them the safe opened with a time lock, and the money could not be reached until ten o'clock, giving time for a raiding party to be organized, resulting in the killing of Bob Dalton, Joe Evans, "Texas Jack," Grattan and Emmett Dalton and several citizens. Bill Dalton, the only member who escaped, organized another gang and on May 23, 1894, "held-up" the First National Bank at Longview, Texas, presenting the following note to the president:

"Home, May 23."

First National Bank, Longview.

This will introduce to you Charles Sprecklemeyer, who wants some money and is going to have it

B. & F."

After the president read the note, he found Dalton

BOB DALTON.   GRATTON DALTON.

Dalton Bros. Band. Bank and train hold-ups—Southwest.

42

pointing a rifle at him, while a confederate stole $2,000 from the paying teller's cage and decamped. A posse, who pursued the robbers, killed Jim Wallace, one of the band, the other escaping. Of the stolen money, three ten dollar and nine twenty-dollar bills were new unsigned bank notes and through these Bill Dalton was traced to Ardmore, I. T., and on June 8, 1894, was killed while resisting arrest.

Nearly every member of this gang "died with his boots on."

After the death of Bill Dalton, Bill Cook collected the remnants of the Dalton gang and formed one of the most desperate and notorious bands of outlaws, desperadoes and murderers in the West. The band at various times, including Bill Cook, Jim Cook, Jim French, Bill Doolin, Crawford Crosby, alias "Cherokee Bill," "Buck Wightman," "Columbus Means," Thurman Palding, alias "Skeeter," Joe Jennings, Charles Clifton, Sam Brown, George Newton, Perry Brown, George Newcomb, alias "Slaughter Kid." Charles Pierce, alias "Bitter Creek," Tom Quarles, Elmer Lucas, Lou Gordan, Curtis Deason, Ol Yantis, Henry Munson, "Tulca Jack," Dick Yeager and Zip Wyatt. Bill, Tom, Jim, Lulu and Rose Cook were half-breed Cherokee Indians.

July 18, 1894, Bill Cook, "Skeeter," "Cherokee Bill," Henry Munson, Curtis Deason and Elmer Lucas, "held-up" a Frisco train at Red Fork, Ark. Munson was killed trying to escape, but Deason was captured. The others escaped. Deason was sentenced to a long term in the penitentiary.

FRANK ELLIOTT.
Dalton Gang.

ROBERT ELLIOTT.
Dalton Gang.

44

July 31, 1894, at about ten o'clock in the morning, Bill Cook, Elmer Lucas, Jack Star, "Tulca Jack" and one other rode into Chandler, O. T., "held-up" the Lincoln County Bank, killed a citizen named J. M. Mitchell, who had tried to give the alarm, rode from the town followed by a posse who came up with them and a fifteen-minute battle resulted. One of the bandits, Elmer Lucas, was badly wounded and captured, the rest escaping. Lucas was sentenced to 15 years in the penitentiary.

October 20, 1894, this band wrecked the Kansas City and Memphis express at Corretta, I. T., by throwing a switch running it into a string of empty cars, marched the engineer and fireman to the baggage and express cars, forced the messenger to open the door, but, as the messenger insisted that the safe was locked and could not be opened until it reached its destination, the gang went through the train and obtained about $500 from the passengers. While still engaged in this, a freight train whistled nearby and the bandits fled.

October 23, 1894, at Watooa, the bandits under Bill Cook's lead, drove every citizen to cover and then robbed every store in town.

November 13, 1894, some of the gang led by Bill Cook, "Cherokee Bill" and Jim French, "held-up" a Missouri, Kansas and Texas train, at Wybank, a blind siding, within four miles of Muskogee, I. T., by side tracking the train. They attempted to enter the express and baggage cars, but failing, shot out all the windows in the cars, riddled the sides of the cars and then robbed the passengers.

WILLIAM MINER.

An old time Pacific Coast stage and train robber. Escaped Aug. 8, 1907, from Westminster Penitentiary, British Columbia, where he was serving a life sentence.

November 28, 1894, Jim French and several others at Chrotah, I. T., "held-up" nine people in a store, plundered the store, the bandits retiring without firing a shot.

Little by little, however, at the cost of the lives of many brave officers and the expenditure of a large amount of money, the members of the Cook band were exterminated or imprisoned and after the United States Government had offered $250 each for the capture of these outlaws. November 21, 1894, Jim Cook was sentenced to 8 years in the penitentiary for murder. November 22, 1894, "Skeeter" at Ft. Scott, Ark., pleaded guilty and was sentenced to the penitentiary. February 12, 1895, Bill Cook in the U. S. Court at Fort Smith, Ark., was sentenced to fifty years in the N. Y. State Penitentiary at Albany, N. Y. January 30, 1895, "Cherokee Bill" was captured at Nowata, I. T., after he had started to organize a new band.

Others of these outlaws killed while resisting arrest were Dick Broadwell, Ol Yantis, Charles Pierce, alias "Bitter Creek," George Newcomb, alias "Slaughter Kid," Bill Doolin, "Tulca Jack," Henry Munson and Zip Wyatt.

"Black Jack" McDonald, who was originally one of the Dalton gang, began operations in the Southwest in 1896 with George Musgrave, Bob Hayes, Cole Young, Bob Lewis and Sid Moore, principally "holding-up" general stores and post offices and killing those who attempted to arrest them.

August, 1896, they unsuccessfully attempted to rob a bank at Nogales, Arizona. October, 1896, they attempted to rob an Atlantic & Pacific R. R. train but a Deputy United States Marshal, who was on the train, organized a posse, killed Cole Young and the others escaped without getting any booty. The others were eventually killed resisting arrest, "Black Jack," the last of the Mohicans, so to speak, being killed in Grant Co., New Mexico, in 1897.

"Old Bill" Miner, who escaped from the New Westminster Penitentiary, New Westminster, B. C., August 8, 1907, where he was serving a life sentence for the robbery of the Canadian Pacific R. R. train at Furrer, British Columbia, on the early morning of May 9, 1906, in his early criminal career was one of the most remarkable singlehanded stage and train robbers who ever operated in the far West, always going about his work in a matter-of-fact way, never posing as a bad man, and never taking human life. He never belonged to any organized band of "hold-ups," generally worked alone until later years he picked up others to assist him.

As early as 1869, he served a term for stage robbery in San Quentin, Cal., prison. In 1879, after his release he, with others, robbed the Del Norte stage in Colorado, of thirty-six hundred dollars. An associate, Leroy, was captured and hanged by a Vigilance Committee, but Miner escaped with the booty, to Chicago, then to Michigan, where he posed as a California capitalist, until his money was exhausted when he again returned to Colorado and committed several other "hold-up" robberies.

In 1881, Miner, Jim Crum, Bill Miller and a man named Jones, "held-up" a stage between Sonora and Milton, California. All were captured except Jones. Crum confessed.

48

Miller and Miner were sentenced to 25 years each, Crum to twelve years. Miner was released from San Quentin, Cal., on June 17, 1901, and two years later on September 23, 1903, with two others he "held-up" and robbed the Oregon Railroad and Navigation passenger train No. 6, at Mile Post 21, near Corbett, Oregon. One of his companions was badly wounded. The other was later arrested and both were sentenced to long terms, but Miner, for whom a reward of $1,300 had been offered, was not captured. Miner on September 10, 1904, at Mission Junction, British Columbia, "held-up" the Canadian Pacific Co.'s railway's transcontinental express, securing $10,000 in gold dust and currency. For his capture $5,000 reward was offered by the Government of the Dominion of Canada, $5,000 by the Canadian Pacific and the Dominion Express Co. and $1,500 by the Province of British Columbia. Rewards of $12,800 seems to have had no terrors to Miner, for on the morning of May 9, 1906, he again "held-up" the Canadian Pacific Railway train, this time at Furrer, B. C., the robbers compelling the engineer to uncouple the mail car and ·haul it a mile away, where they rifled it of registered mail. Miner believed the express packages were in the mail car and when he found they were not, he lost his nerve, abandoned the robbery and escaped. Large rewards induced posses to take up the pursuit. The Canadian Constabulary, after a fight in which one of them was wounded, on May 14, 1906, arrested Miner, also his confederates, Louis Colquhoun and Thomas Dunn. Miner and Dunn were given life sentences, Colquhoun 25 years.

BLACK BART.
"Black Bart," the "P. O." 8 stage and train robber of the Sierras.

Miner is said to have originated the expression, "Hands-up," and was one of the first highwaymen to operate on the Pacific Coast.

From 1877 to 1883, stages in the mountains of California were "held-up" by a lone highwayman, always wearing a conical circus clown hat, an old linen duster and a jute bag about his lower legs.

At times, near the intended "hold-up", he would arrange a screen of jute bagging or canvas, placing behind it dummies made of slouch hats on sticks and all so realistic as to readily deceive. While ordering the dummies not to shoot until he directed or there was some sign of resistance, he would request the driver to please throw out the box and mail bags, the "box" being the treasure box or safe of the Wells Fargo Express Co., containing a large sum of money. He was always polite to the passengers, especially to the ladies, and after each robbery there would be a few lines of doggerel poetry, signed "Black Bart, the P. O. 8." This and the handwriting showed the lone robber to be of more than ordinary intelligence, well bred, and not of the ruffian type.

First a mail coach in the Sierras was attacked, next he would be heard from in the Siskiyou Mountains, on the old trail into Oregon, and so on, altogether committing twenty-three robberies, and for whose apprehension, a large reward was offered. Only once did a driver get a good look at him and described him as an American, fifty years of age, with long gray hair, thin face, deep set eyes, prominent teeth and somewhat dignified appearance.

51

The only record of "Black Bart" being shot at was on November 3, 1883, between Milton and Sonora, in Tuolomne County, about three miles from Copperopolis, Cal., on the old mail road from Yosemite. On this particular trip, McConnell, the stage driver, allowed a boy of the neighborhood, who had a gun, to ride with him, but the lad got down just before the stage was stopped and had gone into the woods. The robber who, as the stage approached, as was his custom, had used powerful field glasses to determine if an armed guard was aboard, as he "held-up" the stage asked the driver what had become of the man with the gun. The driver told him the truth, but as "Bart" started off with the boxes and mail bags of gold valued at forty-four hundred dollars, also five hundred and fifty dollars in coin, the boy returned and McConnell snatching the rifle from him, fired four shots at the retreating robber, but failed to hit him.

Immediately after this, as well as after "Bart's" other robberies, detectives promptly explored the surrounding country, this time near a camp fire, finding a slouch hat, silk handkerchief and a linen cuff with blood stains upon it, the cuff having on it a laundry mark. This was the first real clue and resulted in the detectives finding the San Francisco laundry that had placed the mark on the cuff and determining that it belonged to one E. C. Bolton. The arrest and identification of "Black Bart" followed. He was also known as Charles E. Benton and Charles E. Bowles, had lived at an unpretentious boarding house in San Francisco, passing as a mining man and which accounted for his oc-

FRANK SHERCLIFFE
Lone Highwayman. Train bank and Faro bank Robber.

casional absence. He pleaded guilty to his last robbery, but strenuously denied that he was the "Black Bart" who committed the others and declared to the Court that it was only urgent necessity that drove him to commit this crime. On November 17, 1883, he was sentenced to six years in the prison at San Quentin, Cal. He originally came from Decatur, Ills., where he had worked on farms, and from where in Company B, 160 Illinois Regiment, served three years in the Civil War. He was known in his regiment as "Wrestling Charlie," and so far as could be learned outside of his "hold-ups" had led a respectable life, was a teetotaler, a man of fine education, a remarkably good story teller and since his release he has been seen more or less in honest occupations on the Pacific Coast.

During "Black Bart's" criminal career he never took a life or injured a human being.

———

Early in the evening of November 4, 1892, at Omaha, Frank Shercliffe, alias Sherman W. Morris, boarded a Sioux City and Pacific Railroad train, and as it neared California Junction, Iowa, completely disguised with a false beard, he attacked William G. Pollock, a New York diamond merchant, with a bag of shot, until it was broken open, then seriously wounding him in the arm and shoulder with a revolver ripped open his vest and stole therefrom unmounted diamonds valued at twenty thousand dollars, signaled the train to stop, and escaped.

As a result of our handling the matter for the Jewelers' Protective Union, Shercliffe was arrested and tried at Lo-

The only record of "Black Bart" being shot at was on November 3, 1883, between Milton and Sonora, in Tuolomne County, about three miles from Copperopolis, Cal., on the old mail road from Yosemite. On this particular trip, McConnell, the stage driver, allowed a boy of the neighborhood, who had a gun, to ride with him, but the lad got down just before the stage was stopped and had gone into the woods. The robber who, as the stage approached, as was his custom, had used powerful field glasses to determine if an armed guard was aboard, as he "held-up" the stage asked the driver what had become of the man with the gun. The driver told him the truth, but as "Bart" started off with the boxes and mail bags of gold valued at forty-four hundred dollars, also five hundred and fifty dollars in coin, the boy returned and McConnell snatching the rifle from him, fired four shots at the retreating robber, but failed to hit him.

Immediately after this, as well as after "Bart's" other robberies, detectives promptly explored the surrounding country, this time near a camp fire, finding a slouch hat, silk handkerchief and a linen cuff with blood stains upon it, the cuff having on it a laundry mark. This was the first real clue and resulted in the detectives finding the San Francisco laundry that had placed the mark on the cuff and determining that it belonged to one E. C. Bolton. The arrest and identification of "Black Bart" followed. He was also known as Charles E. Benton and Charles E. Bowles, had lived at an unpretentious boarding house in San Francisco, passing as a mining man and which accounted for his oc-

Miner is said to have originated the expression, "Hands-up," and was one of the first highwaymen to operate on the Pacific Coast.

———————

From 1877 to 1883, stages in the mountains of California were "held-up" by a lone highwayman, always wearing a conical circus clown hat, an old linen duster and a jute bag about his lower legs.

At times, near the intended "hold-up", he would arrange a screen of jute bagging or canvas, placing behind it dummies made of slouch hats on sticks and all so realistic as to readily deceive. While ordering the dummies not to shoot until he directed or there was some sign of resistance, he would request the driver to please throw out the box and mail bags, the "box" being the treasure box or safe of the Wells Fargo Express Co., containing a large sum of money. He was always polite to the passengers, especially to the ladies, and after each robbery there would be a few lines of doggerel poetry, signed "Black Bart, the P. O. 8." This and the handwriting showed the lone robber to be of more than ordinary intelligence, well bred, and not of the ruffian type.

First a mail coach in the Sierras was attacked, next he would be heard from in the Siskiyou Mountains, on the old trail into Oregon, and so on, altogether committing twenty-three robberies, and for whose apprehension, a large reward was offered. Only once did a driver get a good look at him and described him as an American, fifty years of age, with long gray hair, thin face, deep set eyes, prominent teeth and somewhat dignified appearance.

BLACK BART.
"Black Bart," the "P. O." S stage and train robber of the Sierras.

Miller and Miner were sentenced to 25 years each, Crum to twelve years. Miner was released from San Quentin, Cal., on June 17, 1901, and two years later on September 23, 1903, with two others he "held-up" and robbed the Oregon Railroad and Navigation passenger train No. 6, at Mile Post 21, near Corbett, Oregon. One of his companions was badly wounded. The other was later arrested and both were sentenced to long terms, but Miner, for whom a reward of $1,300 had been offered, was not captured. Miner on September 10, 1904, at Mission Junction, British Columbia, "held-up" the Canadian Pacific Co.'s railway's transcontinental express, securing $10,000 in gold dust and currency. For his capture $5,000 reward was offered by the Government of the Dominion of Canada, $5,000 by the Canadian Pacific and the Dominion Express Co. and $1,500 by the Province of British Columbia. Rewards of $12,800 seems to have had no terrors to Miner, for on the morning of May 9, 1906, he again "held-up" the Canadian Pacific Railway train, this time at Furrer, B. C., the robbers compelling the engineer to uncouple the mail car and ·haul it a mile away, where they rifled it of registered mail. Miner believed the express packages were in the mail car and when he found they were not, he lost his nerve, abandoned the robbery and escaped. Large rewards induced posses to take up the pursuit. The Canadian Constabulary, after a fight in which one of them was wounded, on May 14, 1906, arrested Miner, also his confederates, Louis Colquhoun and Thomas Dunn. Miner and Dunn were given life sentences, Colquhoun 25 years.

49

"CAPT." EUGENE BUNCH.
Southern Express Robber. Killed Evading Arrest.

gan, Iowa, and sentenced to seventeen years in the Fort Madison, Iowa, penitentiary.

He is believed to be the lone "hold-up" man who, during 1892, prior to the attack on Mr. Pollock, robbed gamblers and proprietors of gambling houses in the Northwest, usually entering at late hours of the night, while all were engaged in their games and relieving them of such money as they had on hand.

He began his career as a criminal when a boy seventeen years of age, by robbing a safe at Aurora, Illinois, shot at the officers who attempted to arrest him, but was captured.

Since then he has been engaged in a number of daring robberies in the middle and far West. Like the average professional criminal, he squandered his ill gotten gains, but since his release from prison in 1904, still young, but broken in health and prematurely aged he has married and, seemingly is endeavoring to lead an honest life.

In November, 1888, a United States Express messenger was "held-up" on a train near New Orleans, La., and robbed of $20,000. Investigation proved the robber to be Captain Eugene F. Bunch, alias Captain Gerald, a former newspaper editor of Gainesville, Texas.

Acting with the special officer of the Southern Express Company, and a local official, we finally located Bunch in a swamp near Franklinton, La., where, on August 21, 1892, he was killed resisting arrest.

September 30, 1891, Oliver Curtis Perry boarded a New York Central R. R. train at Albany, N. Y., sawed an opening through the rear door, crawled over the freight to

OLIVER CURTIS PERRY.
Single handed train robber. Operated in New York State.

the centre, covered the messenger with a revolver and stole
five thousand dollars and some jewelry, after which near
Utica he made his escape by cutting the air brakes, thereby
bringing the train to a stop.

February 21, 1892, Perry again boarded an express
train near Syracuse, N. Y., concealed himself on the roof
of the express. car until the train was in motion and then
with a rope fastened to a hook in the roof of the car while
the train was traveling fifty miles an hour, lowered himself
to a window and, covering the messenger with a revolver
ordered him to throw up his hands. The messenger attempted to pull the bell cord, but Perry shot him in the
hand, the messenger following with several shots. Just as
Perry fired his last shot, the train pulled into Lyons and he,
in attempting to escape drove the fireman and engineer from
a locomotive which stood on a siding, started the engine
at full speed, but was followed by railroad employees on
another locomotive, who subsequently overtook him and
after considerable shooting caused his arrest.

On May 19, following he was sentenced to 49 years and
three months in the Auburn, N. Y., State Prison, from
which he escaped October 22nd, but was recaptured in less
than 24 hours. Soon after showing signs of insanity he was
transferred to the asylum for the criminal insane at Matteawan, from which he escaped April 10, 1895, but four
weeks later was arrested by a railroad detective at Wee-
hawken, N. J. This detective had a dispute with the Super-
intendent of the railroad about Perry's capture, killed him
and was hanged in New Jersey for his crime. After his

return to Matteawan Asylum, Perry destroyed both eyes with a saddler's needle and is now a blind raving maniac. Perry was born in Amsterdam, N. Y.; at fourteen was sent to a State Reformatory for burglary; afterwards served a term at Rochester, N. Y., then went to Minnesota, burglarized a store, served three years in the Stillwater, Minn., prison, became a cowboy, returned East and imposed upon religious people by pretending to reform, and finally committed the "hold-up" crimes as alleged.

Bert Alvord, a train robber, was once City Marshal of Wilcox, Arizona, and Deputy Sheriff of Cochise County, said to have been a fearless, diligent and conscientious officer, became a train robber and "hold-up" as he claimed, on account of a reward of $1,000 offered for the arrest of a "hold-up" which he was not able to collect, "held-up" a train and took from the express messenger $1,000 declaring he had earned this money and that there was no other way to collect it, thereafter committing many robberies, but was finally hunted down by the rangers and rurales.

In January, 1902, Alvord joined forces with Bravo Juan, Augustine Chicon and Bill Stiles, Texas and Mexican outlaws, working along the border. Alvord and Bravo Juan were captured in the Sierra Madre mountains of Sonora, Texas, tried and acquitted. Later Alvord and Stiles were arrested for a train robbery at Cochise. Alvord was sentenced to two years in the penitentiary at Tombstone, Ariz., but with Stiles awaiting trial in the same jail on six indictments and thirteen other prisoners on December 15, 1903,

HARRY SCHWARTZ.
While brakeman on St. Louis and San Francisco Ry. with Newton Watt, murdered
express messenger Kellogg Nichols.   Stole $20,000.

broke jail, this being the second time Alvord and Stiles escaped from this prison; on the previous occasion, Stiles seriously wounding the jailer. Alvord was later recaptured and served his time in the Yuma, Ariz., penitentiary and was released during October, 1905.

Kellogg Nichols, a United States Express messenger, was found murdered in his car on the Chicago, Rock Island and Pacific R. R. train, at Morris, Ills., on the night of March 13, 1886, the safe open and $21,500, mostly $100-bills, stolen therefrom. My personal investigation at the time, assisted by Frank Murray, then Chief of Police, of Joliet, and afterwards for many years one of our Superintendents, John T. Smith, Chief Special Agent of the Chicago, Rock Island and Pacific R. R. and other officers developed that Nichols had been shot in the shoulder with a .32 calibre pistol, a kind not used by train robbers, and his brains literally beaten out with a car stove poker, which was returned to the hook where it belonged and where any ordinary criminal would not have placed it after making the use that was made of it.

These circumstances together with being unfavorably impressed with the statements of Newton Watt, baggageman and Harry Schwartz, front brakeman of the train, led to the suspicion that Nichols was killed by either Watt or Schwartz because Nichols by tearing off the mask of the robber had recognized the wearer. The following day on the railroad tracks near Minooka, between Joliet and Morris, where Nichols was last seen alive, was found a mask

FRED WHITROCK, alias Jim Cummings.
Lone train robber. Stole $57,000 from St. Louis & San Francisco express train.
Died recently.

made from the tail of an old coat and which showed evidence of having been torn from the wearer.

Ample evidence of their guilt eventually obtained resulting in their conviction and sentence to life imprisonment. Watt died in the penitentiary, but Schwartz's sentence being commuted by Governor Altgeld, he was released from the Joliet penitentiary, September 2, 1896.

A short distance out of St. Louis, Mo., October 25, 1886, a lone highwayman boarded a St. Louis & San Francisco Ry. train, presented a forged letter from the Adams Express Co., prevailed on the Adams Express messenger to open the door of the car. The robber then compelled the messenger, D. W. Fortheringham, to open the safe and deliver the contents, $57,000, to him, then binding and gagging the messenger, left him lying on the floor of the car.

Robert A. Pinkerton and two detectives from our Chicago office, several weeks afterwards arrested Fred Wittrock, formerly of Leavenworth, Kas., for this robbery, who then admitted that four to five other men were concerned with him in the crime and that to each he had sent a portion of the stolen money; that the robbery was conceived by George Haight, a former express messenger and associated with him was Thos. Weaver of Chicago. Aided by the local police, of his confederates we arrested Weaver in Chicago and Haight in Nashville, Tenn., two of Wittrock's friends in Leavenworth and two in Kansas City, to whom Wittrock had given some of the stolen money and a Chicago printer

who printed the forged letter head. We recovered 90 per-
cent of the stolen money.

Wittrock, Haight and Weaver all pleaded guilty and
were sentenced to long terms in the Missouri penitentiary.
Wittrock served his sentence, returned to his old home in
Leavenworth, Kas., and died quite recently.

———

On the Mineral Range Railway, Michigan, at 9:30 A. M.,
September 15, 1893, at a crossing in the woods, called Boston, in a sparsely settled country, masked men boarded the
locomotive and express car and forced the express messenger to deliver to them a package containing seventy thousand
dollars in currency, the pay roll of the Calumet & Hecla
Mining Co. As there was no telegraph office at Boston, an
alarm was not given until the train reached Calumet, when
the local authorities were notified and arrested Jack Butler,
an ex-convict, and Jack King, at that time the champion
Cornish wrestler of the United States.

For the American Express Company, I took charge of
this investigation, going with the manager of the company
and several assistants to the scene of the robbery. Our
investigation assisted by the local authorities showed that
the robbers had used a horse and buggy to escape with,
and of which we obtained a good description from the
natives thereabouts; also a close examination of the foot
prints of the horse, showed he wore racing plates, instead
of the usual heavy shoes worn by horses of that section.
This horse was subsequently identified as "Camp K," the
property of a Red Jacket, Michigan, saloon-keeper, from

CHARLES J. SEARCEY.
Aquia Creek, Va., Express Hold-up robber.

whom the "hold-ups" had obtained it. Our work resulted in the additional arrest of La Liberty, a former railroad fireman, Dominick Hogan, an American Express messenger, and his brother Edward Hogan, who had planned the robbery. La Liberty made to me a confession that the stolen money had been placed in his trunk at the depot, but on searching the trunk we found only eleven hundred dollars. It was then determined that the night depot master at Marquette, Michigan, and a local livery stable keeper had stolen the money from La Liberty's trunk, resulting in my recovering altogether $69,935.00 of the $70,000 stolen.

All of these men were convicted and sentenced to long terms in the Michigan penitentiary.

In the fall of 1895, at Aquia Creek, Stafford County, Virginia, two men, shortly after the train was under way, boarded an express train, one the express car and the other the locomotive, cutting the locomotive and express car from the balance of the train, forcing the engineer to take them a considerable distance where the express messenger was overpowered, the safe blown and over ten thousand dollars stolen, the "hold-up" men escaping, notwithstanding a battle with a posse.

Shortly afterward a stranger displaying considerable money, was arrested at Port Royal, Virginia, from whom Robert A. Pinkerton, representing the express company, who was investigating the robbery, obtained a confession. The robber proved to be Charles J. Searcey, of Texas, and he implicated Charles Morgan, alias Morganfield, whose

PAT CROWE.

arrest we brought about in Cincinnati. Searcey was sentenced to ten years and Morganfield to seventeen years in the Richmond, Va., penitentiary.

During 1902, 1903, 1904 and 1905, several train robberies occurred in California, Colorado and Oregon. The identity of the robbers could not be settled at the time but we eventually determined that they were committed by George and Edward Vernon Gates, brothers of California, who on March 15, 1905, at Lordsburg, New Mexico, with rifles attempted to commit a series of "hold-up" robberies and who killed themselves when the officers attempted to arrest them.

Pat Crowe, notorious as the kidnapper of Eddie Cudahy, son of John Cudahy, the millionaire Omaha packer, for which crime, through a miscarriage of justice, he was acquitted and afterwards acknowledged being the abductor, pleaded guilty to train robbery on the Chicago, Burlington and Quincy R. R. in 1894, about which time there were a number of attempts upon trains in the vicinity of St. Joseph, Mo. Crowe was supposed to have the Taylor brothers of St. Joseph associated with him.

After these robberies we located Crowe in the Milwaukee Work-house, and had him held, charged with a diamond robbery in Denver, Col. Before the extradition papers arrived he sent for the officials of the Chicago, Burlington and Quincy R. R. and stated that he was concerned in the

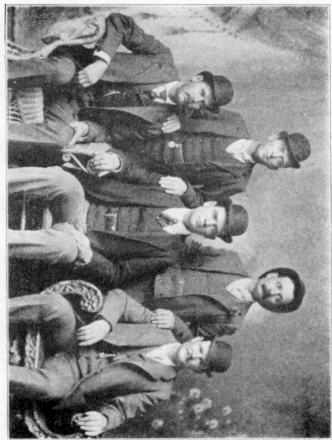

Harry Longbaugh.   Ben Kilpatrick.   "Butch" Cassidy.
              Bill Carver.   Harvey Logan.
                        THE WILD BUNCH.

robberies near St. Joseph. Certain parts of his story appeared very improbable to me and I went to Denver, made arrangements with the police authorities to permit him to plead to these train robberies in Missouri. The night the arrangements were completed, Crowe escaped from the jail. Crowe, after his escape, wrote me that all the statements made by him were falsehoods. Later we caused his arrest in Cincinnati. He was taken to St. Joseph, Mo., where he pleaded guilty and was sentenced to three years in the Missouri States Prison at Jefferson City, from which he wrote letters to the railroad officials and myself, threatening to kill all who had to do with his prosecution.

When his sentence expired in Missouri, Crowe was returned to Denver for the diamond robbery, but through friends it is claimed he compromised the matter.

Crowe has lately written a book telling how he committed some of his crimes. He claims he now intends to atone for all the crimes he ever committed by demonstrating to the young the folly of criminal life.

He was lately tried for robbery in Council Bluffs, but acquitted.

One of the most notorious bands of train robbers and bank "hold-ups" who operated in the West and Southwest, from Wyoming to Texas from 1895 to 1902, was known as "the Wild Bunch." After each robbery they would hide in the "Hole in the Wall" country of Wyoming, and after the excitement had blown over would return to their headquarters in small cities of Texas.

This band from time to time included Tom Ketcham, alias "Black Jack," leader, who was hanged at Clayton, New

HARVEY LOGAN.
alias "Kid" Curry.
of
"Wild Bunch."

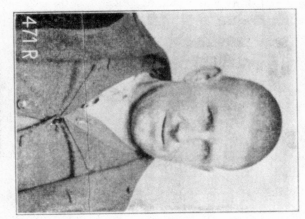

CAMILLA HANKS.
alias Deaf Charlie.
of
"Wild Bunch."

71

Mexico, April 26, 1901, for killing Sheriff Edward Farr, of Whalensburg, New Mexico, who was attempting to arrest him for a train "hold-up."

William Carver, alias "Bill" Carver, second leader, killed April 2, 1901, while resisting arrest in Texas for a murder committed at Sonora.

Sam Ketcham died June 24, 1900, in the Sante Fe, New Mexico, penitentiary, of a wound inflicted by a posse of officers attempting to arrest him for the robbery of the Colorado Southern R. R. Co. at Cimarron, New Mexico.

Elza Lay, alias McGuinness, is now serving a life sentence in the Sante Fe, New Mexico, penitentiary for participation with "Black Jack" Ketcham in the Cimarron train robbery.

Lonny Logan and Harvey Logan, alias "Curry brothers." Lonny was killed at Dodson, Mo., February 28, 1900, while resisting arrest.

George Curry, alias "Flat Nose George," third leader, killed near Thompson, Utah, April 15, 1900, resisting arrest by a Sheriff's posse.

Bob Lee, alias Bob Curry, now serving a ten-years sentence in the Rawlins, Wyoming, State Penitentiary, for the robbery of the Union Pacific train at Wilcox, June 2, 1899.

Among the bank and train robberies committed by the "Wild Bunch" in recent years were: Butte County Bank, member American Bankers' Association. Belle Fourche, South Dakota, June 28th, 1897.

Union Pacific Express train "hold-up," Wilcox, Wyoming, January 2d, 1899.

BEN KILPATRICK.
of
"Wild Bunch" Band.

LAURA BULLION.
of
"Wild Bunch" Band.

Union Pacific Express train "hold-up," Tipton, Wyoming, August 29th, 1900. About 1900, after these robberies, under the leadership of Harvey Logan, alias "Kid" Curry, the band included O. C. Hanks, alias "Camila" Hanks, alias "Deaf Charlie;" George Parker, alias "Butch" Cassidy; Harry Longbaugh, alias "Sundance Kid;" and Ben Kilpatrick alias "The Tall Texan." A part of this band on September 19, 1900, at the noon hour, "holding-up" the officials with rifles and revolvers, robbed the First National Bank, Winnemucca, Nev., a member of the American Bankers' Association, of $32,640 in gold.

July 3, 1901, Logan, Cassidy, Longbaugh, "Will" Carver, Ben Kilpatrick, "Deaf Charlie Jones," alias Hanks, at Wagner, Montana, "held-up" a Great Northern Express train, securing $40,500 of unsigned bills of the National Bank of Montana, and the American National Bank of Helena, Mont., and for which Ben Kilpatrick, alias "The Tall Texan," was arrested by the police in St. Louis, Mo., November 5, 1901, with a number of the unsigned stolen bills in his possession. He was sentenced to fifteen years in the Columbus, Ohio, penitentiary, since transferred to the United States Penitentiary at Atlanta, Ga. In Kilpatrick's room of the Laclede Hotel, the police arrested Laura Bullion, a companion of Kilpatrick, as she was leaving with a satchel containing several of the unsigned bills. She was convicted of being an accomplice and sentenced to two years and six months in the Missouri Penitentiary, at Jefferson.

December 13, 1901, at Knoxville, Tennessee, two policemen who attempted to quiet a pistol fight over a game of pool were shot by one of the participants, a stranger who

GEORGE PARKER.
alias "Butch" Cassidy.
of
"Wild Bunch."

HARRY LONGBOUGH.
alias Sundance Kid.
of
"Wild Bunch."

75

afterward "held-up" the occupants of the saloon, backed out of the rear door and jumped thirty feet into a railroad cut, but was eventually traced and arrested in an exhausted condition from cold, exposure and injury from his jump. We subsequently identified this man as Harvey Currey, alias Harvey Logan. Logan was convicted and sentenced to a term of twenty years in the United States Penitentiary at Columbus, Ohio, for uttering bank notes stolen at Wagner on which notes the signatures had been forged. On November 29, 1902, while awaiting transfer to that institution, he made his escape by "holding-up" the guards in the Knoxville jail; fleeing to the mountains on horseback. He has not been recaptured.

O. C. Hanks, alias "Camila" Hanks, of Texas, another one of this band, in Nashville, Tenn., on October 27, 1901, offered a merchant one of these notes, circulars describing which had been sent by us broadcast throughout the United States. The merchant became suspicious and telephoned the police who responded quickly, but Hanks, noting what occurred, quickly drew a revolver, "held-up" the officer temporarily, jumped into an ice wagon and forcing out the driver drove rapidly down the street; abandoned the wagon and at the point of his revolver captured a buggy and in this escaped through the marshes to the Cumberland River, where he forced two negroes to row him across in a boat and was lost trace of.

On April 17, 1902, he was killed by officers in the streets of San Antonio, Texas, while resisting arrest. In 1892, Hanks and Harry Longbaugh "held-up" a Northern Pacific train in Big Timber, Montana, for which Hanks was ar-

ETTA PLACE.
Mrs. Kid Longbough.
of
" Wild Bunch."

WILLIAM CRUZAN.
of
"Wild Bunch" Band.

BOB LEE.
of
"Wild Bunch" Band.

78

rested, convicted and sentenced to ten years in the Deer Lodge Penitentiary, from which institution he was released April 30, 1901, rejoining his old companions in "hold-up" robberies.

"Butch" Cassidy with Harry Longbaugh and Etta Place, a clever horsewoman and rifle shot, fled to Argentine Republic, South America, where they, it is said, have been joined by Logan. Being expert ranch men they engaged in cattle raising on a ranch they had acquired, located on a piece of high table land from which they commanded a view of 25 miles in various directions, making their capture practically impossible. During the past two years, they committed several "hold-up" bank robberies in Argentina in which Etta Place, the alleged wife of Harry Longbaugh, it is said, operated with the band in male attire. We advised the Argentina authorities of their presence and location, but they became suspicious of preparations for their arrest, fled from Argentine Republic and were last heard from on the Southwest Coast of Chili, living in the wild open country.

———

Edward Estelle, alias "Conn. Eddie," George Gordon, alias "Brooklyn Blacky," William Browning, alias "Browney," Thomas Clark, alias "Pa. Butch" and Johnny Bull, all "yegg" men, on August 5, 1902, "held-up" a train of the Chicago, Burlington and Quincy R. R., near Marcus. Ills., after subduing the engineer, fireman and conductor, and shooting up and down the railroad track to intimidate the passengers, secured three thousand dollars from the Adams Express Company's safe in the baggage car.

79

THOMAS CLARK.
Yegg Express "Hold up."

GEORGE GORDAN.
Yegg Express "Hold up."

George Gordon, alias "Brooklyn Blacky," approaching from the front of the locomotive was mistaken for a railroad man and shot in the thigh by Estelle, who, when he discovered he had wounded a member of the gang, endeavored to have Gordan flee with him, but on the latter pleading that he was too badly wounded, Estelle, uttering an oath and telling him that he would not be left to squeal on anybody, blew Gordon's brains out and then wanted to burn Gordon's body in the fire box of the engine, which Clark prevented.

We identified Gordon's body, found on the railroad tracks and this materially aided us in establishing the identity of the others of the "hold-ups." We located the gang at Memphis, where, acting with the police, we arrested Fstelle and Clark. Browning, alias "Browney," was shot and killed at McCloud, Texas, while attempting to rob a bank, the owner of which took Browning's pistol from him, killing him with it. Clark and Estelle were sentenced to life imprisonment in the Joliet, Ill., States Prison.

A gang of "yegg" men "held-up" a through train of the Illinois Central Railroad near Harvey, Ill., on the night of August 1, 1904, with revolvers, compelling the passengers to deliver their money and valuables. These "hold-ups" were traced to a St. Louis lodging house by St. Louis and Kansas City police detectives, who arrested one man as he left the house. The detectives on entering the house to arrest William Bruce Morris and Albert Rosenauer were attacked by these criminals and a fierce battle ensued. Both criminals were killed but not before they killed Detective

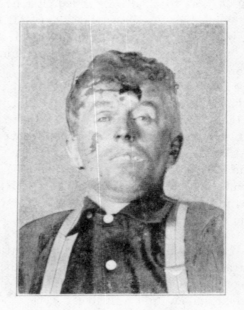

WILLIAM BROWNING.
Yegg Express "Hold up."

John J. Shea and Special Officers Thomas F. Dwyer and
James A. McCluskey. Morris in an ante morten statement
confessed to the Illinois Central "hold-up"; also to an attempted "hold-up" of a Chicago, Rock Island and Pacific
train near Leets, Iowa, July 29, 1904.

Although the "hold-up" men have usually been successful
in their "holding-up" of stages, trains and banks, there have
been occasional instances where the "tables were turned" on
them.

One of these was near Gilliam, Missouri, shortly after
midnight, Sunday, December 26, 1906, when a lone robber,
who had boarded the train at Slater, Mo., compelled the
sleeping car porter and the train conductor to accompany
him through the cars, the porter awakening the passengers
in the Pullman sleepers, collecting their valuables and hand-
ing them over to the robber. As the train reached Glasgow,
Mo., the next stop for the train, the robber disappeared, but
while the conductor was reporting the robbery to a telegraph operator, the "hold-up" by signal to the engineer
started the train, although the conductor succeeded in having
it stopped and informing the engineer of what had occurred
started through the train, when he met the porter, the flagman and the "hold-up" man, who under the "hold-ups"
direction were continuing to relieve the passengers of their
valuables. The robber again forced the conductor to become a member of the "hold-up" party. On reaching the
last car, the "hold-up" locked the flagman and porter in the
ladies' toilet and started to take the plunder from the flag-

man's hat. Elias B. Haywood, the conductor, watching what was occurring, found the "hold-up" robber off his guard, grappled with him and both wrestled about the car floor, but finally the robber released himself from the conductor's grasp and disappeared out of the door on the platform, the conductor firing several shots after him with the robber's revolver which the conductor had captured during the struggle. The conductor believed the robber had jumped or fallen from the train which was running at forty miles an hour, but on going on the car platform, found the "hold-up" man crouching on the lower steps, gave him a severe beating, pulled him back into the car and held him until the train pulled in at Armstrong, Mo., where the police, having been notified by the Glasgow operator, were in waiting.

The robber gave his name as Jesse Clyde Rumsey, and claimed that his brother "held-up" the Chicago passenger train near Glasgow, Mo., on November 8, 1906, at which time a similar robbery was committed, and from whom he received his instructions how to operate.

What I have maintained that no crime pays and that 95 per cent of criminals die in debt and frequently in want is most aptly illustrated by the history of the "Hold-up" Robber."

I know of few train robbers or "hold-ups" alive and out of prison to-day. Only in a very limited number of instances are these in comfortable circumstances and from honest means only after giving up their lives of crime.

Crime does not pay!

POPULAR CULTURE IN AMERICA

1800-1925

An Arno Press Collection

Alger, Jr., Horatio. **Making His Way;** Or Frank Courtney's Struggle Upward. n. d.

Bellew, Frank. **The Art of Amusing:** Being a Collection of Graceful Arts, Merry Games, Odd Tricks, Curious Puzzles, and New Charades. 1866

Browne, W[illiam] Hardcastle. **Witty Sayings By Witty People.** 1878

Buel, J[ames] W[illiam]. **The Magic City:** A Massive Portfolio of Original Photographic Views of the Great World's Fair and Its Treasures of Art . . . 1894

Buntline, Ned [E. Z. C. Judson]. **Buffalo Bill;** And His Adventures in the West. 1886

Camp, Walter. **American Football.** 1891

Captivity Tales. 1974

Carter, Nicholas [John R. Coryell]. **The Stolen Pay Train.** n. d.

Cheever, George B. **The American Common-Place Book of Poetry,** With Occasional Notes. 1831

Sketches and Eccentricities of Colonel David Crockett, of West Tennessee. 1833

Evans, [Wilson], Augusta J[ane]. **St. Elmo:** A Novel. 1867

Finley, Martha. **Elsie Dinsmore.** 1896

Fitzhugh, Percy Keese. Roy Blakeley On the Mohawk Trail. 1925

Forester, Frank [Henry William Herbert]. The Complete Manual For Young Sportsmen. 1866

Frost, John. The American Speaker: Containing Numerous Rules, Observations, and Exercises, on Pronunciation, Pauses, Inflections, Accent and Emphasis . . . 1845

Gauvreau, Emile. My Last Million Readers. 1941

Haldeman-Julius, E[manuel].The First Hundred Million. 1928

Johnson, Helen Kendrick. Our Familiar Songs and Those Who Made Them. 1909

Little Blue Books. 1974

McAlpine, Frank. Popular Poetic Pearls, and Biographies of Poets. 1885

McGraw, John J. My Thirty Years in Baseball. 1923

Old Sleuth [Harlan Halsey]. Flyaway Ned; Or, The Old Detective's Pupil. A Narrative of Singular Detective Adventures. 1895

Pinkerton, William A[llan]. Train Robberies, Train Robbers, and the "Holdup" Men. 1907

Ridpath, John Clark. History of the United States, Prepared Especially for Schools. Grammar School Edition, 1876

The Tribune Almanac and Political Register for 1876. 1876

Webster, Noah. An American Selection of Lessons in Reading and Speaking. Fifth Edition, 1789

Whiteman, Paul and Mary Margaret McBride. Jazz. 1926